Volume 80 of the Yale Series of Younger Poets

Pamela Alexander

NAVIGABLE
WATERWAYS

Pamela Alexander

Foreword by James Merrill

YALE UNIVERSITY PRESS
New Haven and London

This volume is supported by a grant from the National
Endowment for the Arts.

Designed by Nancy Ovedovitz and set in Goudy Old Style
type by Composing Room of Michigan, Inc. Printed in
the United States of America by Vail-Ballou Press,
Binghamton, New York.

Library of Congress Cataloging in Publication Data

Alexander, Pamela, 1948–
    Navigable waterways.
    (Yale series of younger poets; v. 80)
    I. Title. II. Series.
PS3551.L3574N3 1985   811'.54   84-40666
ISBN 0-300-03331-1
ISBN 0-300-03397-4 (pbk.)

The paper in this book meets the guidelines for permanence
and durability of the Committee on Production Guidelines
for Book Longevity of the Council on Library Resources.

10   9   8   7   6   5   4   3   2   1

for John Tagliabue

CONTENTS

FOREWORD

> A series of white squares, each
> an hour's flying time, each with instructions
> in pencil: the organized adventure. . . .

Pamela Alexander's book begins with a map, one whose arbitrary divisions recall pages of manuscript. The poem is dedicated to Amelia Earhart; its subject and way with scale may well be courtesy of Elizabeth Bishop. Poet and pilot are both given to flights. And while never saved by a stanza as provably as by a well-drawn chart, we readers feel at home with the analogy and come to see in those white squares the very building blocks of experience: units of space, time, energy, information. "Like quickened days," Alexander presently tells us, they "take turns showing her senses/what to do." (Another poem will speak of "the glass doors between my days.") Such chambers, forever varying in substance and dimension, are vital to her world.

The poet-pilot "renews / herself, like the engine, for / one thing. Flight. . . ." During a brief earth-walk she joins

> a crowd of Javanese walking up a volcanic mountain.
> They laugh and talk, they carry baskets
> and various loads on poles. . . .

Random detail? Not really, with its overtone of spiritual quest and the resonance of "poles" whereby the weave of those baskets mimics that of longitude and latitude, as in primitive models of the globe. That people carry their worlds uphill with them she *doesn't* say, doesn't need to—continuing instead to trust her imagery. The map which underlies this whole poem now brings it to an end, along with Earhart's life, as

> The plane staggers with the weight of fuel,
> becomes lighter and then
> light. The last square has

an island in it, but cannot
lead her there.

A rhymed, concluding couplet lies in wait for us here. So does a
sense of Flight from which legerdemain has abstracted the initial F
(present also, from the start, on the fuel gauge). Any child learn-
ing how to spell can play this sort of scrabble. To quicken a poem
with it, however, ear cocked for the hidden thoughts of language,
calls for temperament and skill in no way childish. As the Warburg
Institute's motto puts it, God Lurks in the Details.

Under a microscope there are lights in a leaf
that flicker and go out, as the leaf dies.

The least chamber in her poems is found to contain and emit
energy. Present now as the star in a bedside carafe, or "nightjar,"
now as that bird itself with "wingbars like lights shot / from a
wave," this innermost quantum fuels the self, renews it; also, in
ways a mystic would understand, effaces it:

She wonders what holds her life together.
Not herself; she too is held.
Something does it like daylight through
a glass of water.

Given such diffidence, or such faith, no wonder that only midway
through the book's fifth poem does Alexander take on the first-
person singular, stepping from the wings with characteristic droll
precision into "the middle of chart 13260, / east of Maine." She is
discovered standing in a sailboat cabin a bird has just flown in and
out of.

This poet works elegantly, unpredictably, without teasing. Her
voice can be wholly direct ("Hey you,"); her subjects—heat, air,
sex, trees, the peerless dog Pfoxer—impeccably democratic. Yet
she is most at home in distance, and the more she offers herself for
inspection, the more cryptic the result is. "Talking to Myself at
27" constructs in paradoxical detail a psychic shadow-box in
which personality is upstaged by cyclical, genetic events. A "line
of little girls" lengthens in the opposed mirrors she studied as a
child. Here

Trying to get my head out of the way
without moving my eyes

was an occupation that gave me numerous headaches
and glasses before I was five. Older philosophers
have gotten worse results
from similar exercises.

Whereupon the poem all but shudders into prose, as if at the tread
of the "large old lady" whom her own grandmother's "ungainly
silhouette" shows Alexander she will become. Then her voice lifts
in wry urgency:

> One thing the mothers and sisters and teachers
> were careful not to mention
> but that grandmothers boldly engaged in
> as if it didn't matter what anybody said,
>
> was dying, walking into
> the empty mirror just out of sight,
> darkening to a silhouette in which someone else
> appears, someone familiar—

It's anything but dull, this minimal view. What we share with
one another, the solo, spotlit rehearsal of human concerns, is
dimmed in favor of structural excitements shared with all creation.
The little girl notices "the grain in desktops," sees in the desk an
"iron-legged comrade, confidante, mentor." The trees in "Scher-
zo" become great floating nightclubs where "green flares go off,
and smallish gongs" and "waiters circulate / with drinks, and wiry
insects perform / skating tricks." Slung between them, a ham-
mock lines its occupant's back "with longitude / and latitude,
tropical waist / to temperate brain." Some cells "tend the ele-
vators / of respiration; others drive sports cars wildly / through
the tumbling blue traffic / of the blood"—the adventure, by now
less "organized" than positively organic, depicting the grain of
one's precious individuality as

> an imitation grain,
> small strokes and walnut swirls,
> intricate as weather patterns
> in a satellite's eye

or, even more openly, unmasking it as

> the imagined person, the one
> made with small strokes

on this paper
that used to be trees.

The small strokes now and then involve more wordplay than
usual in a serious poet's work. Surely *Libretti*, the book's last sec-
tion, owes not just its title to Gertrude Stein's *Operas and Plays:*

IV.
Ivy that is.
Had you forgotten.
X.

Spelt out, the roman numeral becomes a vine; romanized, the past
participle's final syllable imitates two crossing vines, an unknown
quantity, a graphic kiss. Small strokes indeed, but done by a master
illuminator. Again: when is a door not a door? Alexander answers
the old joke with fairy tale logic: instead of *ajar*, a finished piece of
crockery. Notice how "-ful" and "empty" complete and cancel
each other, the way a dark shape prints a radiant afterimage:

A stone jar smoothes with use. Useful.
An open door is empty.

Such effects are dictated by "historical necessity." If World War
I caused, as we hear tell, the total cave-in of civilization except
where it glinted on in the minds of writers like Valéry and Joyce,
the problem for later generations has been to create works whose
resonance would last for more than a season. A culture without
Greek or Latin or Anglo-Saxon goes off the gold standard. How,
then, to draw upon the treasure? At once representing and parody-
ing our orphic wealth, the lightweight crackle of wordplay retains
no little transactional power in the right hands. Of course, it
raises—as for that matter did the gold itself—the question of ill-
gotten gains. Even today, how many poets and readers choose the
holy poverty of some second-hand diction, pure dull "message" in
translation from a never-to-be-known original. "There is no wing
like meaning," said Stevens. Two are needed to get off the ground.

Certain poems, like "The Vanishing Point," to the degree that
they seem constructed upon purely playful impulses, run the risk of
reducing the unsympathetic reader to fury, or the receptive one to
trance. Somewhere along the line Alexander's point *does* vanish,
into the kaleidoscopic symmetries and elisions of the text.

And yet not so. Her scene is a monastery. Her characters include donkeys, doves, monks, and their guests:

> They raise honey bees as well in the alcove,
> the oldest part of the wall.
> Their will is very old. They and we
> arrange straw for the bees in niches some of which are
> occupied also by stone saints.
> The bees are particular since
> the straw creates their cloisters.

Here still are chambers, lodgings of energy: the dovecote, the hive. As the last hypnotic bells (well/wall/will) fade away, a flat, unmusical sentence concludes the book:

> Finally we forget what we are carrying and do not
> make mistakes.

Rest in action? Faust's solution, or the saint's. But a specific echo, too. It would have us turn again to the opening poem, where holiday-makers were carrying baskets on poles up a mountain, and where a navigational "mistake" sent the pilot to her death. The poet, surviving, casts this backward look, austerely nonchalant, which puts the world in its place: for her purposes, the printed page.

James Merrill

ACKNOWLEDGMENTS

Anima: "Talking to Myself at 27"

The Antioch Review: "In the Room Next to Yours"

Ardis Anthology of New American Poetry (Ardis Publishers):
"Flight," "Air"

Exploring Life through Literature (Scott, Foresman and Company):
"Flight"

Field: "Vines"

Poetry: "Tea Story"

Poetry Now: "Portrait with Beast and Omnibus," "The Way
Down"

The United States in Literature (Scott, Foresman and Company):
"Air"

Grateful acknowledgment is made to Harcourt Brace Jovanovich
for permission to quote from Amelia Earhart, *Last Flight* (1937)
and to the University of Hawaii Press, for permission to quote
from Hajiwe Nakamura, *Ways of Thinking of Eastern Peoples* (An
East-West Center Book, 1964).

Special thanks to the Fine Arts Work Center, where many of
these poems were written, for its support; also to Juli Feigon, Tom
Sleigh, and David St. John for their comments on the manuscript.

PARTS OF A GLOBE

Flight

For Amelia Earhart

A series of white squares, each
an hour's flying time, each with instructions
in pencil: the organized adventure. "Carelessness
offends the spirit of Ulysses." She suspends herself,
as he did, in the elements, finds
reason turns to motion, caution to design.
"One ocean led naturally to
another." Earth led naturally to sky
after a look at a thing of wood and wire
at the state fair in Des Moines, after the sting
of snow blown from the skis of training planes
near Philadelphia.
                    The rumble of the red and gold
Electra wakes the air, shakes stars
down their strings until
they hang outside the cockpit, close enough
to touch. Squares, like quickened days, take turns
showing her senses

what to do. The fragrance of blooming
orange orchards carries to considerable
altitudes. "No one has seen a tree
who has not seen it from the air, with
its shadow." Lake Chad is huge, shallow,
brightened by the wings of cranes and maribou
storks. The Red Sea is blue; the White and Blue Niles,

green; the Amazon delta a party of currents,
brown and yellow, distinct. Beyond

the clutter of sensations, the shriek and clatter
of tools at landing fields, she renews
herself, like the engine, for
one thing. Flight
above the wine-dark shining flood
is order, makes the squares
come and go, makes the plane
a tiny gear that turns the world. "Of all those things
external to the task at hand, we clutch
what we can."
                         She leaves the plane briefly to join
a crowd of Javanese walking up a volcanic mountain.
They laugh and talk, they carry baskets
and various loads on poles. "Sometime
I hope to stay somewhere as long as I like." For

the last long passage she abandons personal items,
souvenirs; also the parachute, useless over the Pacific.
The plane staggers with the weight of fuel,
becomes lighter and then
light. The last square has
an island in it, but cannot
lead her there.

Tea Story

"that Excellente & by all Physitians approved Chinean drink"

1. Twining, Thomas. Teaman. Devereaux Court, Temple Bar

> returns from the forests of Assam
> in which he verified the Tea shrub to be
> indigenous, abundant, and virtually
> inaccessible. At noontime on the upper deck he brews
> an ordinary Canton cup; salt tempers its oils, discolors
> the spoon. The backs of his hands shine.
> The Quaker captain
> nods twice a day. Afternoons,
> Thomas visits the Thibetan goat, the ten curious sheep
> from Santipore; he looks for cracks or seepage in the
>   lacquer
> of oil tubs, checks the fleet of crates—cheated
> of tea, they carry tortoise shell, jars of green
> ginger.
>   Sweet evenings,
> it is not the mild vegetable infusion of his family's name
> to which he turns to soothe the tick of unused muscles
> before sleep, the cabin's tilt and tilt
> about the hammock's axis; he downs
> a glass or two, another few,
> and tinkers with the fates of friends, acquaintances
> he has not seen these thirteen years.

2. 9 December 1795

> Stood out of the estuary, just
> afternoon; junks

hoisted baskets of exploding crackers, gongs
talky at our going. The constant stir of water is
a second silence. The men are calm; sleeping
without blankets, they perfect
our vulnerability. I balance, idly, old
accounts—the Fox & Geese, Hampstead: 7 chests pekoe,
                tincture of rubarbe, sugar in loaves. &
                for Sundries Forgott.—and write odd
letters: a faster ship may pass for them.

                                    Around Good Hope,
heavy weather, a hundred ducks
drown in the hold. Now
I keep to my cabin, a pint
of bitters. In all this wash it comforts me
to see sharp things, the nice
strokes about the elephant's ear
in the aquatint I have for you. I am uneasy
at whales. Algae thickens: we must be near

belled towers. Squares.
Oh solid and to be praised
stone gates, meadows, your estate.
At night an abundance: yellow, white
windows.

Portrait with Beast
and Omnibus

The paraphernalia required
to take the turn-of-the-century photograph
must have been considerable
but common enough
that no one is paying much attention
to the contraption on the beach
—most of the secondary figures show
as backs of hats, or
backs. The donkey, of course, is
disinterested, head half out of the frame.
It is the style of his species
to be undisturbed
by messiahs or machines, whatever
their reception by another genus.

In the two dimensions
of the brown and white photo
printed crooked on a post card,
the woman seems to be wearing
the building behind her as a hat: two large
arched windows and cupolas—
one louvered—of a streetcar station
frame her head
as a pagoda does a sitting saint.
Under the brim is a fringe
of tassels, which are distant women
in long skirts on a curved sidewalk
going to meet the next car.

With bare legs dangling
around the donkey's barrel,
two children stare at the mountainous

camera on command; their histories pause
in their held breath. A hand
on one shoulder of each child
like parentheses or white
halves of a prayer, she stands
behind durable beast and passengers,
pointing the latter in the direction
of their inscrutable futures
while other people hurry up the street
to catch theirs
and the century turns a corner
of its own invention.

A Marriage of Sorts

The maze is round and blue and green.
Clouds float over it,
and feathered ounces fly—
ouzels, loons; their cries sound
like miniature wine-glasses breaking
against the crusty earth.
The birds are white flares starting
from dark trees and viny swamps
as if in celebration. But what
festival is here? Are the droplets flung
from the hands of drowning men
tossed in joy like rice at weddings—
the worthless coins with which
they try to buy their breath back from the sea;
are their last cries
choked with gladness?
                         The globe is lovely. Colors
fit together in intricate designs
that wash away, and form again;
the planet in its veil of weather
wobbles, bright and dark. Clouds
and birds and cries
rise and turn together, fall.
Dissolving, they make circles
within the circles of the seas.
And land circles sea in
an ancient sort of dance.

Story with Ornament

God and the author knew
where the mice got the motorboat,
but they had it and some
confidence in finding their way
based on a hat with tea roses
they mistook for a chart.
The blooms were bodies of water;
stems, navigable waterways.
I remember a picture of the important hat,
concerned mice
crowding around it.

The vignette is both
brief incident
and running ornament, originally
leaf or grape, appearing
throughout a text.
Hence the bird, which flies quickly
into my mind and out again
several times a year.

The further we move from stories
that explained the world to us as children,
the more the images silt in, become
imbedded in our lives
and the lives of lovers,
friends. Boat,
lamp, sky, bird,
are no longer abstract.

Shall I take you for a sail,
sister? The boat you helped me buy

is old and strong. Shall I take you
flying, one wing in water, the other in air,
skating on the seam
between ocean and sky?

Years ago a bird flew into the cabin
of the sailboat where my two friends
were sleeping,
circled cleanly in the small space
and flew out again, past my face
into fog, and night, and the rush and bubble
of the fat boat pressing through
wave and wave and wave
in the middle of chart 13260,
east of Maine.

Now the wind picks whitecaps
out of the black water
between our boat and the power plant.
From its stacks, tipped with red lights,
fine black grit sifts downward.
We recognize ourselves as Adults
from our children's books, the ones
who seemed to know what they were doing.

The wind that meets the body of the sail
and curls against it, a few feet up,
is stronger than the wind on deck.
Water is less easily displaced
at the bottom of the propeller's circle
than near the surface. Most distinctions
are gradual; clear-cut ones appear
in fairy tales and in the colors
on the chart. White.
Turquoise. Tan.

How many stories have I heard
or read in thirty-five years?
They begin to remind me of each other;
the images vignette, shade off

into the ground that is my own
story.

I have been anxious to know
where I am going.
It is slowly occurring to me
that it doesn't matter, or it's too late,
or the question is irrelevant.
We are moored here
in Salem Sound
taking spray on deck, the boat
bucking and water creaming at the bow
without our going anywhere
but a few feet up, a few feet down,
and some weaving back and forth.
We read aloud to each other.
We tell each other stories about our childhoods
lived in the same house
six years apart.
We listen to the wind, read some more
in the cabin lit with candle lanterns.
I sleep
lightly, and in my dream
the bird flies into the cabin
and makes one circle, the shape
of the world, the shape of a hat,
the shape of the stories we make of ourselves
asleep, awake.

The Way Down

I

All her instruments read zero.
The cockpit is filling with water.
She crawls onto the fuselage, knowing
it is done, the flight she started from New York
and another one as well. Lying on the plane's tinny
wing, hollow as the bones of a bird, she looks up
at the last cloud she had fuel to fly through
and tells herself: it's a warm night,
don't shiver.
    The tail tilts up and she slips
into the sea, her leather jacket heavy instantly.
When she knows it is time to take
a first last breath of water
she makes it deep,
writhes

and loosens,
sways down through colored
layers to the mud. White
crabs and bottom-feeding fish
take back the miles, one by one,
and seaweed twists in wreaths around
the rusting struts and bright wings
she rode down.

II

My arms try their reach
toward books on upper shelves
instead of stars,
but I am drawn

by the pilot at the bottom of the sea.
I want to remember her
gently, find
her lack of fear, shape
my years into a flight
that embraces the world
and let go only when
there is no other way.
Before what is myself becomes
stiff and glazed, I will
talk to myself, to you; we are
falling together.

INTERIORS

A Canvas Glass

Your sister's sitting for you Vuillard
intérieur. jeune fille assise
among the plants and her hands are empty
intérieur. rouge et gris

She looks straight out of the colors Edouard
intérieur. bleu et vert
The house is a frame. She doesn't go out
intérieur. fenêtre ouverte

The leaves in the print of her dress can't drink
from the window's glass of air.
The blind lets in light in bars you can see;
she's clear as yourself Vuillard

In the Room Next to Yours

Plaster drops from the long thin boards
into my shoes at night.
I like seeing bare laths, the truth
of how a house hangs on. What did I think
walls were? I saw only
costume, paper wrappers over
the stuff of them.

Nothing could disguise the catastrophe
of your bed. It clanked, it rattled,
it shrieked: it must have had
moving parts, like a heart.
If we had slid underneath and looked up
—what mysteries! All the machinery
of a pre-Copernican universe, whirs and wheels,
clicks and clutches, pulleys and bearings and

brakes. I know there were brakes.
The underparts of the bed must have been
as intricate as the rituals you had
in the morning, the ones you had at night,
to keep away fires, and lightning, and hurt.
They didn't work.

I was afraid of your fears and left you, trailing
loose clockworks. What did I think
a love was? Through the wall
I hear a new one moving.

Lights They Live By

1. nightjar

A carafe beside her bed or a glass goose;
a piece of water, stoppered, or a solid chunk, like ice?
She watches it all night,
death, the brightening star.
She thinks it is one with her all along
or she thinks it is the final thing she contains.

She reads all night.
Under a microscope there are lights in a leaf
that flicker, and go out, as the leaf dies.

All night.
Cities of lights.
A glass of water has as many.
The smallest piece of water has lights in it,
she reads, and looks
at the carafe to find
a juggler tossing jugglers holding stars.

She is a maze. She finds a candle at each
corner but loses the way. She thinks
she can make it up as she goes, strike
a bargain, make it stick.
Or she thinks she can't,
turns again.

She wonders what holds her life together.
Not herself; she too is held.

Something does it like daylight through
a glass of water.

She has a son. He cuts his hands in grass,
long grass that leads to the sea.
He listens to water.

She has a song for him, tells him
the first ladder was a fern; she shows him the lines
that craze a leaf, says she's not, he's not
out of the woods yet, praise be.

2. daybreak

Whatever he sees in his hands is beautiful.
He sees lines; stones; lumps of glass, often
(often they are green); a carved cat; he sees
the last day of his life.

Looking closer doesn't change things.
Through a magnifying glass obsidian is still
glossy, like a muscle; a moth's wing
porous as manila paper.

He thinks he could put a bottle together in his hands
if he had all the pieces. He looks
for them, stands

waist deep in grass among the dull
green lamps of fireflies, hundreds, below
night-hawks flashing their wing-bars like lights shot
from a wave.

Days open and fold. Geese
slide through them, French curves.
The hawks shriek and turn;
they are pieces.

His rooms are a forest of things that have
touched him, including a jar
of rain, a pair of marble pigeons.
He picks up some white glass to give it away
and keeps it.

His hands tell him everything. They ache
when a friend he desires turns away. Still
he thinks he can find and keep them
all, all his days.

The Catacombs Again

As you were.
What are you looking at now.
I'd imagined you too long, made a hieroglyph
of your bright hair.
You came and were gone.

A scenario: the grey birds and the white birds
adjoin each other like words.
Adjacent.
The roots of thousands of plants press against the walls;
inside on the walls all my friends are dancing together.
If one is gathering facts
these are merely adjectives.
Regardless.
The failure of not having seen is nothing like
the failure of not having looked.

The verb "to come."
How did you know about caves?
You knew where I would come and gave me a prophetic
look.
The book about caves is filled with pictures,
words and pictures, the moving cat
in several positions.

The leaves of a vine or a sentence.

I suppose we are adjacent if you want to
go that far.
I have rented a burrow for the winter;
if it were a donkey I would ride to see you.
My words were sent

to see you;
the rest of you is left to read the book,
the birds,
the walls.

Two Places to Live

"There is no left or right without remembering."—Gertrude
Stein

1

You return like a new moon, lost friend found, you
build, retreat; a glacier. Coarse & steaming
caribou rummage over it, leaving tracks the size of
dinner plates; beneath its creaking mass, forests

bruise to coal. Yet you pass lightly through
the glass doors between my days, as easily as the sea
lifts and carries its tonnage of ice-shapes, that
broken alphabet. Right hand meets left: as often

you come, from countries in the sea & continents
of snow. Where I live, the woods bloom thinly,
black and white. Still, there are tracks. Still
the branches empty of your weather, and fill.

2

Plants pull light through the windows, save it up.
He keeps pennies and birdseed in pots. In other rooms
men sing loud as cossacks carousing in their socks.
They drink to the rowdy sun. A yellow bulb

of liquor warms in his hands; he rubs them dry
on flannel sleeves. Outside, with practiced shrugs,

ducks adjust their plumages, which are white
purses nearly translucent in the sun. He adds ice

to his glass. Doing things one by one keeps days
apart, keeps him from stopping on the roominghouse steps,
forgetting to go in. He thinks: the clutter of ducks,
the plants, are forms of sunlight, smaller lights.

He thinks if he remembers everything, everything
will fall into place—the men, the drunken words they
    sing.

Fish Fact

for Carolyn

Two fish
alive, strangely, in air
lay fat and heavy,
one in my hands and one in yours,
and looked peaceful,
happy, even.
We hadn't caught them;
shiny and solid,
they materialized
as we sat in the dinghy
in a harbor
under the wide sun,
looking at each other,
good friends.
What I remember
after falling up the familiar darkness
that always surprises
at the end of sleep
is that they were different:
yours had stripes
and mine was mottled.
So the meaning that follows me
above the surface of sleep
(the meaning, always less
than the dream)
is that we are different,
in the middle of all we share, and that
we can be peaceful with that fact,
happy, even, in our strangely
shining lives.

Primer

for Ed

Look at the birds in the tree,
you said. It sounded like a sentence
for children learning to read.
We drove toward the tree.
The starlings lifted as one
and printed, on the white sky,
a second tree beside the first.

The trees I am looking at now
are blue ones on the white china cup
warm in my hands.
The radio is tuned between stations
because the fizz helps me think,
blurs the voices that rise
through the wooden floor.
Sometimes they are children's,
cutting through wood and static
like the cries of herring gulls.
What? Why? Why?
Why do they ask so many questions?
Why do you ask such hard ones?

There were no curtains
in this small room by the sea.
A roll of glazed, white paper,
meant to wrap wedding presents,
instead protects my privacy, tacked across
the four windows. They bleach sunlight
to the color of flour.

The grove of blue trees
surrounds a pool of coffee,

black like roads in cities
and birds in wet spring trees.
It sounds like a story
children learn to read from,
words forming slowly in their minds
next to their images
of tree, road, bird.

Covered, the windows are screens.
On one of them I see us driving
under a sky streaked with birds.
You are careful of my privacy,
and your own; the questions,
infrequent anyway, stop
if you see I feel pushed.
They ask me
to make the globe in my head
a good place to live.

Words can form maps
to make the world clearer.
I care about you.
Birds hidden in the china trees
fly up in a blue stream.
When I go into the day
they color the sky.

Talking to Myself at 34

Some wood lightens with use: paths
I walk through these five rooms
are the color of grain—
wheat, let's say, for its productive
connotation. The staff
of life, however, is work
enjoyed.
Some wood
darkens with sweat, smoothes:
ax handles, slender and delicately curved.
Leaned against a shed
somewhere in my childhood,
the axes were taken in at night
to keep them from rust
and racoons. The latter
craved salt left
by the sweet work of humans
who craved the work.
Chips from my grandfather's blade
were thick, uniform
and hot in my fingers.

Hey, you,
is this where we're going to live?
Worn wood house, floors
gone honey-colored, dark
doors. A city house
since it was built, although
the city wasn't always urgent
(trucks shake the walls, sirens
rattle windows): once

only hoofbeats
on hard sand, carriage springs
squeaking.

The blonde wood of the doors
is painted with an imitation grain,
small strokes and walnut swirls
intricate as weather patterns
in a satellite's eye.
Every door in costume,
a few understudies stacked
in the basement.
Hey, you.

When I was in grade school
I looked at things
more slowly.
I noticed the grain in desktops,
put out my hand
to each new iron-legged comrade, confidante, mentor,
as if to introduce myself, felt
its surface, rubbed smooth
with the rubbed spines of many books,
the same book over and over,
but different students reading differently.

Hey, you,
in an old house
with tools that want to be used.
A few cracked windows. Outside them,
cars and radios and shouting people
make a city.
Inside, I discover the door's duplicity
by looking at wood carefully for the first time
in years. Real wood
made into imagined wood.

So the you I'm calling to,
the you that is me,
the one who wants to tell me
everything I know,

is both real and invented,
the woman whose name is on the front door
and the imagined person, the one
made with small strokes
on this paper
that used to be trees.

Two Pieces

Since no semantic connection between questions and answers is required [in Chinese], the answers can be of infinite variety. Question and answer are given in a moment. —Nakamura

1. She is pleased to see them in the passage

   A pier glass as a conjunction.
   3 glasses in a line.
   Looking out   looking back   looking out.
   She holds up stones to see
   them glossed, pitchers of milk, porcelain,
   quartz; herself among them.
   Beyond the sills the white clay hills appear
   and do not   appear:
   a partial view of the cliffs.
   Hills of china,
   hills of france. She
   compares, holds & beholds
   earthenware   paper trees   a wood duck   decoys.
   The glass is in her hands, her eyes. The vase
   contains voices, her own
   among them.

2. She is puzzled and reflects a moment

   A bottle is a breakwater; an eye holds
   a shotglass of the light the world sees.
   Her image flashing for an instant in his gaze
   shatters but recurs, a surface looking in.
   A linear impression: a hand-painted piece, perhaps

Limoges. A long time.
These fragments frame a question. A

broken mirror breaks again: cracks,
flawed glass.
The figure in the glass returns at length.

Inside Story at the Asylum

Come for tea,
chickadee in the evergreen; clear green tea.
How long. Oolong.
Music on the porch.
Foxtrots on the lawn. The stems of the mint
are as square as the steps. Come.

Comfortable. A white cloth.
Cream tea, sugar tea, round. Steep
steep tea and light brown light.
Earl grey watercolors, glazed
clay urn.

The azaleas are lovely. Why
be one? People do that, put colors on. Why be
jasmine tea drinking.
Among the bittersweet bushes
people keep talking and drinking.

I watch the easiest one.
Someone at ease is at home, his house is
anywhere a capital letter made from
the air about him. An initial,
what is the rest.
The house of air vibrates in the sun: his voice
unfolds, a bird unperching.

Things keep going away.

We two make a system, water and land.
A shore is an assurance,
it moves a bit but it stays.
I see you, his look says, open
as the air that holds us both. Some water

34

is ice; people do that too, go cold and hard.
Everything does. Transparent puzzles

are difficult to assemble, the mind's
a delicate subject he says.
His words fall down like pebbles, a lot of letters
he puts together and throws away.

Things go away, no one can keep
a river around.

The last of the mint-light light from
the big elm lamps.
The last of the glossy ice, yellow tea, the last
taste taken at the angle
at which birds brake.
He goes. Come again. I see
a G clef shatter
in the empty glass set down.

NATURAL FORCES

Air

It holds us, gently,
together.
It presses out, against the eardrum.
It presses in. It curls
in the palms of our hands

but holds nothing
to itself. It steps over
the sock flung onto the chair, the blouse
on the floor. When we touch,
it moves aside—a modest medium

that solid things displace.
The children running down the street
punch through it, leaving
a cut-out shape of each position
hovering behind them
for an instant.

It is made of round
spinning things, but
it will adjust to a rectangular space such as
a room.
It's the only company
the old man who stays in his long underwear all day
has.
He comes onto the porch at noon
to get more.

People identify it by objects it surrounds.
They call it "atmosphere."
What people see is
themselves: they approve or they don't,

they leave for good or they come back.
Air is innocent of such judgments, having
no personality to protect.

It has
a simple habit:
it fills anything.
It occupies entire hotels
in the off season.

It is drawn to emptiness as to
a question it answers. Only a person
can puzzle it: the vacancy interior,
locked behind the eyes.

It stays whole, flows around
the wall, the knife.
We can change it
as much as ourselves, or
another person:
very little.

Heat

It clings to us,
a loose but unshakeable
garment, transparent
plumage, a thin
atmosphere to our far-flung
colonies.

We share it
with whatever we touch.
When we hold each other,
our clouds combine:
suddenly we are hot,
kicking off the covers.

Ambitious,
it rises above its source—
ourselves or the furnace
in the cellar. A wedge
of warm air eases

up the stairwell,
as determined
in its migration as geese
in theirs;
nestles in the point
of the ceiling.

The primary source
is the spendthrift sun.
Our floating particle, the earth,
inherits a merest fraction
of the sun's largesse.

It is a magnificent
allowance. Ask

the old woman in the solarium, humming to her cat.

The need to keep our temperature
within a narrow range of comfort
affects the shapes
we call culture:
buildings, clothes are made
to protect or dissipate the warmth
within them. Hats, even; rooftops:
riding above a person or town
like accent marks above a line of letters,
they are as much the language
as their bearers.

Heat lingers about our heads,
halos for mortals.

Forced to give us up, it will
vacate the outermost provinces
of hands and feet,
gather in the fist
of the heart.

Sometimes we seek escape, dive
into the sea, drink iced tea in the shade
of the plane tree.
We can only modify it.
It is as easy to discard
as our lives.

Absence Absinthe

Absinthes two absinthes. I did not press upon you.
A tendril, yes; confessed.
Contentedly. We ate carefully then we drank.
Two feasting forward.

Does it please you, our tendency
to keep distances between us? When we don't
look at each other we think we are closer, which
is why the gods don't watch us. The intervals
among them and you and me
are musical. I took
some last looks and now
you can resume.
A field of perfect clover: reasons
are not needed and there are several.

The flowers of wormwood are yellow or white.
The flowers of anise are yellow or else white.
Two dark green oils one
bitter one sweet. Absinthes
two absinthes. A couple is two.
One and one or
one and another
make what? Our glasses touch.

A Well-Known Elizabethan
Double Entendre

If we are dying, let's do it slowly, together.
Are dolphins ever tired?
The way we have been leaping
about the steamship *Intercourse* and heaving
as if it ran on our hot breaths;
the way we have been yelling
as if our lungs were bellows for the furnace
of that gentle, violent vessel;
the way we gasp and clutch each other
like drowning sailors, then die to find
another life, ourselves transformed
and kissing easily as fish or playing
like dolphins over waves,
or tossing like the waves themselves
above the sea-bed, after
having beaten around our respective and
respectable bushes
on dry land for so long—
I am turned around, not sure
if we are found or foundering.
There is a storm above the waves
and one below, but for all our
sweet struggle, the churning all around,
our sporting in the wake,
the ship appears to be more or less
on course. We sight a new world daily.

Hamilton Spring

I stand where the water will part.
Only a diver or a dolphin
will see the hull from here
after the boat is launched.
The bow strokes upward, sharp
as a steeple, smoother than a sail, precise
as a mathematician's thought.

Beech leaves don't mat like oak leaves.
They stay light and whole through the winter
and now they rustle, salting spring
with an autumn sound.

This is about woods.
Hamilton is not particularly important.
It happens to be here.
It's a place I'd never heard of
until I came here to work on a boat,
miles from the sea.
I find it good to start
from a place I don't know.

My friends in Austria were attracted
to the birch forest silvered in mist;
they got a little lost, a little happy,
wandering and talking.
Then they saw a tank. Two tanks.
And men with rifles, very still.

Your eyes look past me.
I see in them a frozen lake,
a few trees.
I want to be something to you.

The dog is out of sight;
out of hearing, even. I want
to make a difference for you.

We look at pictures
of the boat being made.
Fiberglass in a mold, it was one piece
like a need.
Needs are vectors; they point
and push.
Wants are more diffuse,
care less about getting to the point.
They might have no point at all
or several.
Wanting is negative, something
absent, an open space.

The puncture from the thorn doesn't bleed
although it seemed deep.
Because of the beech leaves, I can hear
the dog disappear.
Trees change as we look at them.
The light between them and us
changes too.

We sand the hull cleaner.
White dust shoots from the electric sander
and drifts from handheld sandpaper,
aging us through the afternoon.
By six we are gray.

Wooden silhouettes of tanks and soldiers
were propped against trees
in the story that started
in the Austrian woods.
And then there were real soldiers,
very young, with cheerful faces,
who made sure my friends had a watch,
told them the war games
would start at two o'clock.

There would really be shooting.
They should be sure to leave.

One field away from the boat in its cradle,
the dog curls up, brown bush
among bushes.
I run a thorn hard into my finger
as I untie her.

Now you look out your kitchen window
and your hands do nothing in the sink.
You look out on the lake
that exists only at the back of your eyes.
I am walking in the woods
around the lake, meeting
the many women, men too,
who love you.

Yellow beer and light gray trees.
The crisp shape of the hull,
primed now, white, waits for color, poised
on its stiff wooden wave, beamy
in its cradle.
And the dog runs the anchor line
around four bushes, maybe five; enough
that she can't move. I'll have to untie her.

In Provincetown we walk up a dune
that has buried the trunk and branches,
and stand at the top of a tree,
are for the moment
heavy birds, see the buds
that will open late this year
and for the last time.
The path is narrow and fenced with nettles.
Farther into the dunes,
tips of branches show
a few inches above the sand
in roundish constellations
that were leafy crowns.

Here I come. I say it
so as not to startle you
in the rooms of your quietness
where you can forget I am in the house
because you are thinking.
Solitude can be constructive,
necessary.
I have it too,
a place simply apart,
not withheld.
A cool place to swim, the water
tinged to tea
by oak leaves.
Here I am.

Deep, deep in the woods,
past loneliness, past
the part of the forest we can see at all,
the dog is lost; to us, not herself,
like a person beyond thinking.
Animals go there and don't notice.
They press through the dim green light,
their paths opening only as they pass.
I've seen waves open like that
for the keen shape of a boat
and shut again, and be the same.
There is nothing to be done about
most things.

Pardon me, but you do have
just the right amount of hair
on your chest and arms.
You are really pretty.

Baking steams my windows white.
I don't expect any one thing
to happen. I concentrate
on not wanting;
a double negative,
a space surrounding a space

like the plains upon plains
of the sea.
I have only a few wants and
I can keep them or give them away.
I will love you as I do
certain landscapes. Shallow hills, say;
a few thickets.
Nothing alarming.
Don't be afraid.

We needed coffee.
The store was a long way back.
Dry grass stabbed our feet,
and I fell behind.
You said quietly, "I think it's best
to ignore it." I was just able
to do that. I had to work at it.

People don't make people happy.
They are or they aren't.
You don't seem to mind much
either way.
I guess it isn't particularly
important. It happens to be there
or not, like this town or that, this wave
or another. An old friend
calls all of this,
boat, dog, trees, soldiers,
he calls it
"passing the time."

For Sylvia, For Us

So much is aimless. Her poems are
taut, high-pitched; like a scream,
yes. And she had had enough of living.
When I was fifteen, reading one of her last
poems for the first time, she was dying.
Daffodils by the thousands, bees
in their sticky houses, wax and heavy—
these could not save her.

                    Taut, a bowstring:
the idea that tore through
her mind, as if shot from a terrible cupid—
that death would solve what marriage, what
children, had not; that women sacrifice
themselves, half-willing victims of marvelous, discreet
malevolence—magnetized a hundred troubles
to point to it: the coldest winter
in years, the electric strike's
blackouts, even the stars
pointed that way
in a mind made up,
in an instant.

                  Let us not
agree. Let us go to the Devon house next spring and see
daffodils bloom, bees swarm; skim cream
warm off blue milk, make the horses sweat
with running.

His Own Weather

1. Inside

The cat's fur warms quickly;
the pads of his paws take
longer. The air he has left outside
looks damp, a layer of diffuse waves
above the dense ones in the bay.
A snowflake snaps
its complicated parts together
in my mind; the snow I think will fall soon

is already falling, invisibly high.
The cat makes himself neat
on the sofa, tucks his paws under
like a package beginning
to wrap itself. Self-contained,
he has his own weather
indifferent to the first flake
emerging from its tall cloud. Neither of us
sees it slide
down the long frozen cliff of air and melt
on the shoulder of a wave.

2. Outside

Cats become more visible
after a snowfall.
They pick their way through the wet streets
like old people;
they avoid the white lawns.
It has snowed for days, the double-sided waterfront
crackling with ice, ducks taking to deep water.

Snow blooms in window-boxes.
All the cats in Provincetown are sitting on fences
watching three days of snow become four.

Each flake has miles to fall, takes
hours; sometimes it flies upward in the wind.
The cat sits at the bottom of the air. Flakes
stand in his fur and do not melt.

When it is not snowing the cat watches
everything that moves.
When it snows he watches what doesn't move:
the spaces between flakes. Trees.
The spaces between trees.
When he runs into the spaces, he is still.
Streets, houses, snowflakes, people
fall past.

The Dog at the Center
of the Universe

Husky-masked, bologna-tongued, Pfoxer
settles her bulk on the bed and props
a long jaw on the window sill
like the muzzle of a pioneer's rifle,
heavy to hold alone; pivots it
as she examines the gestures
of grass and birds. The universe,
itself created expressly for her perusal,

is putting the finishing touches
on an August dusk.
Red light slides up
shafts of grass, hesitates, then
springs; the luminous tips blink dark.
The field cools and ticks like an engine
just turned off. She scans it
not for Indians but for rabbits,
those fascinating creatures
with ears so like her own—long, soft,
alert. Surely rabbits and she have interests
in common, issues to discuss with little fear
of disagreement! But the difficult cousins
have so far fled her well-meant attention
and all invitations to play.

She sighs. She closes her eyes and allows
her weight on this side of the fulcrum
to swing her face toward the moon
—rabbit-light, muse to whom she sometimes
raises voice as well as nose.
I would not care to wager

53

that she does not register some delicate
moon-scent
in that moist, oversized chemical analyzer
that is the furthermost point of both
her physical construction
and her sensory appreciation
of the above-mentioned universe.

Her paws work in a dream. She shoots
after rabbits, or moons.

Muzzle-loader, she slams
her own dinner home; lifts
that magnificent sniffer
to consider my choice of spices
for the soup; longs to get my dinner
in her sights, too.

Talking to Myself at 27

I agree.
The house plant plagiarizes the field of
wild flowers; imitation
is inevitable.
My mother at 27
was probably looking at her *Pittosporum japonica*
and talking to herself.

She married late; I was born
when she was 41. It's never too late
to put the self together
with parts of other people, to become
a piece of the world they likewise
possess.
"My daughter is . . ." she tells her friends.
"My daughter is two; she's learning to talk;
I've taught her every word she knows."

The world can continue to exist only by
repeating itself. In Magritte's *Plagiarism*,
made in 1960 or about twelve years after
myself, a field of flowering bushes grows
inside the silhouette of a potted plant,
species unknown but a late bloomer
no doubt. We late bloomers tend to be
self-effacing.

I have sisters. I have teachers
who are also women.
I grow up
as in a convent. The *japonica*

has white flowers, waxy, well
protected.

Two mirrors hang on opposite walls
of the small attic room. In one,
I see my pigtails and blue corduroy dress
in alternating front and back views
12 or 21 times
depending on what year it is
and how well I've learned to count.
The line of little girls
curves out of sight, but I'm sure
it's endless, like numbers.

It was an arrangement Tantalus could have traded
for his pears and pool
with no other gain than
a change of scenery.
Putting one eye in the proper position to see
myself multiplied *ad infinitum*
meant my head got in the way (I have since
found this to be the main reason
infinity remains undisturbed).
Trying to get my head out of the way
without moving my eyes
was an occupation that gave me numerous headaches
and glasses before I was five. Older philosophers
have gotten worse results
from similar exercises.

There are other mirrors.
I will fill the ungainly silhouette
of my mother's mother, the one
who showed me I would never grow up to be
a little old lady, that I will become
a large one instead.

My future still curves like the arc
of eighteen little girls
and exhibits the same perversity: leaned into, it
disappears. But now I know it is concealing

56

something more interesting than repetition.
It ends.
One thing the mothers and sisters and teachers
were careful not to mention
but that grandmothers boldly engaged in
as if it didn't matter what anybody said,

was dying, walking into
the empty mirror just out of sight,
darkening to a silhouette in which someone else
appears, someone familiar—
a girl running through a weedy field,
a woman watering a house plant
and muttering—
someone almost
the same.

The Garden in the Middle

Panes and eggs make fragile dozens:
two times six in cardboard nests, food
for angels who eat cake; three
times four the membranes between weathers.
Frames hold themselves in wooden hugs
that keep the world together, the glass
a cubist with twelve angles on what is:
peach tree; sea flexing; perhaps a house
being painted blue. Here, a Q:

a british line. A dozen people
wait to buy beer in the sculpture garden.
English sparrows and leaves also
stand in lines together, higher
than the humans. Big plants
digest sunlight and rumble in their juices.
People through the queue sit
to tea-cakes and quiches
at tables made of metal imitating
lace: ornate with curlicues,
the iron legs are painted white
as eggs. Dozens of dozens of windows
surround the lines of this and that:
the museum looks out, and in,
at its informal center. The courtyard

a disordered game board:
tables white squares, flagstones grey, both
scattered crazily. Couples
play hearts everywhere. Queens and
pawns and wandering knights take cues.
Jokers coin jingles

and wink. Second fiddles
fiddle with their drinks. And hundreds
of visions of the light touching things
pass through the tiny panes of eyes each
instant.

Hands hold the light up
as they gesture, conducting
conversations. When
the people in the garden talk, they are
what they say. When they are quiet
their bodies are maps of the cosmos,
hands five-pointed stars. Fish dive in the blue
streaks of their arms, angels rise
in their smiles.
Rings and bracelets flash like waves
landing, waves fragile
as glass, as white shells washed ashore.

Figures: Herring Cove

Gulls sit about with straight faces
as though they are not surprised
to walk on water, as though
they were here the last time
the bay froze, a hundred years ago.
They rise and squawk and fight
above the floes or ride them
in neat lines; as smart, in their white
uniforms, as miniature
midshipmen.
       They should review
their charts, for half the fleet
lies jumbled on the beach—great blocks
like broken numbers dropped
from some celestial computation
rounded off.

       These
grand pianos, polar bears, salt
barges, the sea's spare syllables
packed in ice—all have a second shadow:
melting, they etch their images
into the beach.
       Surely
after their sailing drills are over
sea birds study the prints
of dark and prodded sand, short
-lived fossils of a slight
ice age; for recognizing the instant
at which drip and drip and drip combine
to fix a figure in the sand

is an exercise for mystics, the reverse
of seeing through a rainstorm to
its single drops, through
a rising flock
to its composite flights.

The beached hulls are shoulder high
but sinking, unbuttoning their gray crystals
one by one and loosing them, carelessly,
like small talk; dissolving, topside,
into mist.
                    Here you and I
are rudely upright figures; we walk
among the non-commissioned battleships
on which the warm air has designs
of reducing to row-boats; look, we are
strung with them along an abacus
—with these gull-crews, ice-boats,
this watery slip of a globe,
we are sliding toward a sum

who yet work our own passages
through the wheeling world.

LIBRETTI

Vines

A.
Acacia. flowering and an archway.
A round ambush = an abyssinian cat.
Consider lines as small events:
a curled cat uncurling.
Consider events as places to live, and
            paragraphing
                        as paper sculpture.

A polygon has many angels.
How many cousins to the ounce?
How many weasels to the once?
Consider the shapes breath makes: words   clouds
coins in the blood
florins.

A flourish.

II.
Two parts. Often it does.
mountain and river.
First loss lasts
and fills itself
with glosses.

B. the glass blower.
His breath closes open air, makes
spaces into shapes.
Bottles   clear or amber
a green glass
a blue dress:
he says can I look at them all
all at once.

Eyes
small rooms to hold worlds   cities, woods
and the wide shadows of words travelling toward the sun.
She says may I look at you.

IV.
Ivy that is.
Had you forgotten.
X.

Winter a white angle.
A gable.
Gabriel at the table, upon it
is oil.   precious.   pressure.
In a brown bottle a crush of prehistoric fern.

V.
The leaves he showed her became the first she'd seen.
She is a shape in space containing many things;
where his eyes burned her there is
room for tigers
            the Tigris

        irises
        one ibis

        two.

The Biography of a Tree

is not like that of a building which
is structure on crutches. The sails of the woods
were awake.
Deeper than rivers forgotten
dearer than trees and bushes
clear like the music of the birds
of the forest of light,
bright like the fur of bees or of foxes in the snow
and like the deer that come and go,
not falling not holding on we steadily
meet.
Coming and going is neither perfect nor poor, the sails
of the forest are open and

green. A frond a friend
a fern uncurls.
Pleased to be pleased.

A *Fur Piece*

for Teresa who saw the cat cross the street to get to the adage

a likely story. The cat in the first sentence
resembles a small bush. a pond filled with reeds.

On the terrace
Teresa with a bunch of fruit prepares to pare.
Waxy scraps construct another fruit upon the floor.
She ponders. Its likeness is half strange.

semiquaver. He crosses quick as that or
quicker. No adage crossed his mind.

 a middle like a C. In the middle of a pounce the cat
 resembles nothing so much as.

a pounce.
The open mind
complicates space into a street, traffic
whizzing by, opaque. The cat merely
goes and comes.

a short play.
He crouches near Teresa who is halving pears, edible
loot. looks as she opens their yellow light.

The fattest cat can fit into the thinnest plot.

 coda. a plausible tale.
 Aphorism at rest, he becomes
 touchstone, for good luck, for bad: a curious
 fact. The cat at the end of the fable
 is just another cat.
 a pond. a shrub.

Landscape with Frame

While he was in New England she was in Blue Earth, MN.

The tomb of Neferrenpet is decorated with birds &
divine cats engraved in red clay, sign
for the flesh. A pfennig for a pint-pot, bright
dead vessel. Gold and beery schooners
casks on board & tankards too
creak toward the feast, new earth: Vespucci you are
in our veins, driving Fords and Fiats.
                                    The Plains
Indians never rode on wheels although they lived
in round tents set in circles, made mounds
(and danced around them) for those whose throats
had shut, in dust, mouths filled at last.
Bison troops, miles of muscle & cagey bone, drop,
done. Each one
a hot heap, cool nickel in
the next round. Of musketry. Of poker.
Of gin. Guns & yellow wolves flash in timber.
Cabins, uneasy, arrange themselves like steps
of a proof, a logarithm raising
the roof of Europe to the power N.
                              Another line of
beasts, camels, come, eccentric,
working bulky knees in starlight, in firelight,
pioneers. The sacred ibis stirs among red
reeds. Scoters & mergansers have been noticed
by the crews of tankers nearing
port. The hulls are heavy:
honey; oil; & coin, the metal
edge of conquest. The new coast the image

of the old. Magi on the glassy desert pass
pairs of herons fishing in the Nile; wooden
saddles pitch like ships
or prairie wagons.
                    The passage,
the long haul: such the sentence
daily. While

he went to Nice and shared reflections with the waves, she
     went
insane, was sent to Pennsylvania a prisoner, an explorer
lost at sea.

Scherzo

She is a mermaid caught in a net,
feet merged into a tail-fin
in one webbed end of the hammock, or
she is a planet hung like a lantern in space.
The cords diverge
and line her back with longitude
and latitude, tropical waist
to temperate brain.
She is an angel lounging
on a stringy cloud, unleavened
cirrus.

Trees hang above her, their globy tops
bushy stars on stalks.
The leaves are busy with
all kinds of commerce and curious
emergencies—green flares go off,
and smallish gongs; there are raucous
goings-on in the palisade layers
where pairs of cells dance between the columns
and odd ones idling along the fibrous walls
look out through leaf-pores
at constellations of leaves,
galaxies of trees. Waiters circulate
with drinks, and wiry insects perform
skating tricks and acrobatics on the waxy decks.
A party! The leaf manufactures
streamers and lights and sweet liqueurs
from the cranky air.

Though she lies lazy as a land mass
between the hammock's polar regions,

nothing within her precincts
is still: while some cells, of quiet
disposition, tend the elevators
of respiration, others drive sports cars wildly
through the tumbling blue traffic
of the blood, or jockey trucks of produce
about the stomach rumblingly; some dash
along nerve paths with telegrams
and holler out *Halloo—halloo—*

                                        She is
a red leaf! suspended between
the stout stems of trees and linked
to the living commotion
by the subtle twig of breath, that
ether
her mind has ridden on for years
like a flock of grey birds circling,
a school of planets swimming.

The Vanishing Point

Perfectly black coffee in a white perfect cup, this
is simpler than flowered towels. The loom of course
makes its own arrangements, adding to line
histories of line, condensing
movement over time
into the short time it takes to see.
The thinking line is design.
Blooms.

Two chinese horses in a carpet.

Two chinese houses amid dim stems.

In the middle of the page is a photograph of a giraffe.
In the gazette, gazelles appear as paragraphs.

We make our rooms by hand: gestures create
the objects around them. The coffee as I mentioned.
Crockery. The stems.
A few vegetables and chairs.
The door is open a crack that is ajar.

He didn't raise hand or voice.

A stone jar smoothes with use. Useful.
An open door is empty.

A man we hadn't seen in years.
His changes made his sameness strange:
he moved us
to another room   out of doors.

A door that is opened isn't one:
a space instead.

A porch has insight like a bay window a glass boat or
bottled water. Inside
the plants consider, we sit with them;
they contain themselves. The broad
shadows of leaves make continents on the floor boards.
An english ivy, a boston fern:
we carry them off the verandah in their pots.
Wide and green, a port.

An open door is not one or two but through.
Openness brought by a stranger we knew.

Out of doors an open room.

2

A pair of donkeys on a red road.
A pair of pairs.
We think the monks are strong like geometry.

How many yellow robes
how many hours.

One in a row.

They sleep parallel like brothers like trees.
They often work in rows
in the hall
    the garden
by the fish
pond, they raise doves in a Roman ruined tower.
To what power does one raise a dove.

Doves are distinguished by pointed tails.
In the dovecote a coterie. a distinguished group.
Doux
doux
doux

the monks have a few for dinner however. A coup.

It is good that what they say disappears like food
or like a beautiful old father.
Shaping pots, weaving cloth: what they make
is plain. Their flowers are in their garden.

Foxglove. The figure of

a dove facing a fox is pointed at both ends.
They have no use for foxes; a brace
of pheasants is preferred.
They raise honey bees as well in the alcove,
the oldest part of the wall.
Their will is very old. They and we
arrange straw for bees in niches some of which are
occupied also by stone saints.
The bees are particular since
the straw creates their cloisters.

Finally we forget what we are carrying and do not
make mistakes.